Great
Hispanics
of Our Time

Henry Cisneros:
A Man of the People

Maritza Romero

The Rosen Publishing Group's
PowerKids Press™
New York

Published in 1997 by The Rosen Publishing Group, Inc.
29 East 21st Street, New York, NY 10010

Copyright © 1997 by The Rosen Publishing Group, Inc.

First Edition

Book Design: Danielle Primiceri

Photo Credits: Cover © Ron Sachs/Consolidated News Pictures/Archive Photos; all other photos © AP/Wide World Photos.

Romero, Maritza.
   Henry Cisneros : strong political leader / Maritza Romero.
      p.   cm. — (Great Hispanics of our time)
   Summary: Focuses on the political life of a Mexican American who realized the importance of good leadership and served as a mayor and cabinet secretary.
   ISBN 0-8239-5082-4
   1. Cisneros, Henry—Juvenile literature. 2. Cabinet officers—United States—Biography—Juvenile literature. 3. Mexican Americans—Biography—Juvenile literature. 4. Mayors—Texas—San Antonio— Biography—Juvenile literature. 5. San Antonio (Tex.)—Biography—Juvenile literature. [1. Cisneros, Henry. 2. Cabinet officers. 3. Mexican Americans. 4. Mayors.] I. Title. II. Series.
E840.8.C52R66 1997
976.4'351063'092—dc21
                                                                      97-7431
                                                                         CIP
                                                                          AC

Contents

Henry's First Lessons

Henry Cisneros was taught by his father and grandfather to love learning and hard work. Henry was born on June 11, 1947, in San Antonio, Texas. His grandfather, Romulo Munguia, had left Mexico for San Antonio in 1926. Romulo became a **journalist** (JER-nul-ist) and a **printer** (PRIN-ter). He wrote about things that were important to Mexican Americans. Henry's father, George, had been a **migrant** (MY-grent) worker. He believed that having a good education could make a person's life better. So he went to school and then worked for the U.S. Army.

▲ Henry used his love of learning and hard work to help cities across the country.

The Best He Could Be

Henry grew up in a Hispanic neighborhood. His parents believed that their five children should work very hard to be the best they could be. Henry and his brothers and sisters had to do chores, study hard, and take piano lessons. The family talked a lot about what was happening in the world. They also talked about their Mexican **heritage** (HEHR-ih-tij). Henry often listened to his grandfather's stories of growing up in Mexico. For fun, the family went to museums and concerts together.

Henry's parents believed that he would be successful. And he was. Henry was asked to work with two presidents. ▲

6

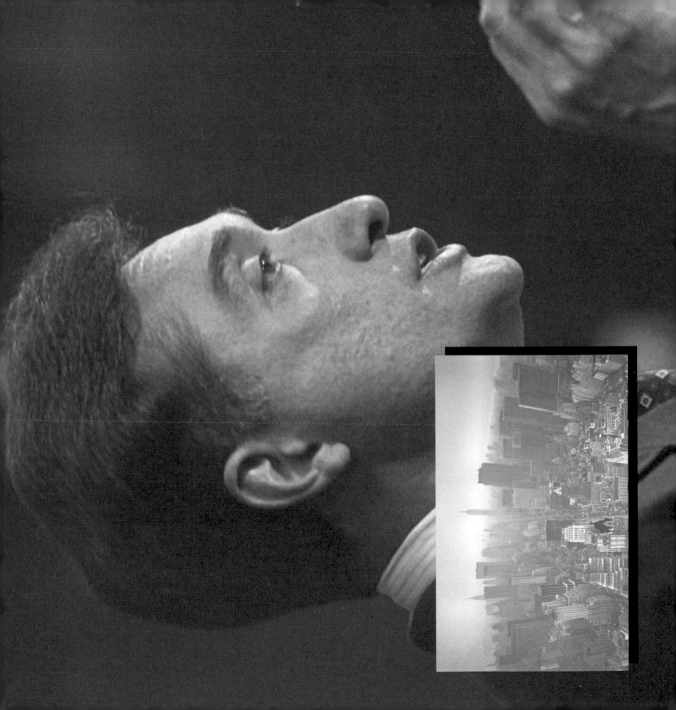

A Good Student

Henry was a very good student. In 1964, Henry went to Texas A & M University. While he was a student there, he took a trip to New York City. It was the first big city he had ever been to other than San Antonio. Henry had thought that he would join the army like his father. But while he was in New York City, he noticed how important good **leadership** (LEE-der-ship) is for the people who live in a city. He thought that he might be able to help his country better by being a leader than by joining the army.

▲ Henry's trip to New York City helped him to decide what he wanted to do with his life.

9

Learning to Be a Good Leader

By the time he finished college in 1968, Henry had decided that he would one day be the **mayor** (MAY-er) of San Antonio. He went to school to learn more about cities. He also worked for a program that helped the city of San Antonio solve its problems, such as bad roads and poor housing. The job taught Henry a lot about what kind of leader would be good for a city. He also learned about the problems of poor Hispanic people in San Antonio.

As a leader, Henry had to learn how to speak to reporters and large groups of people.

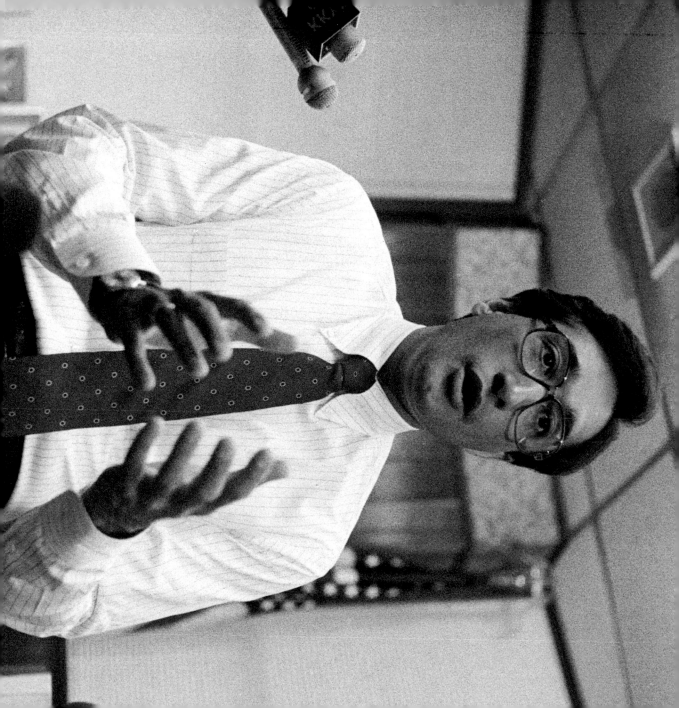

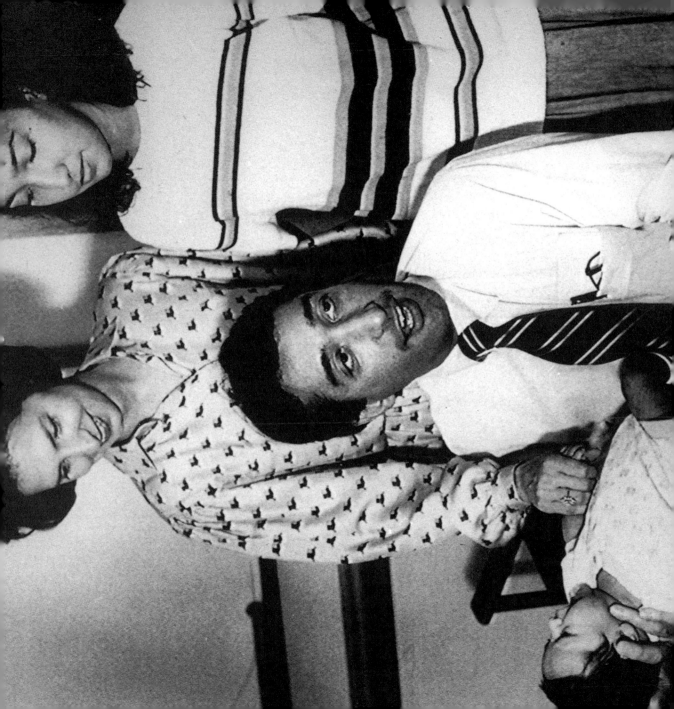

Learning About Politics

In 1969, Henry married Mary Alice Perez. They moved to Washington, DC. Henry was going to school to learn how to be a city leader. In 1971, he worked at the White House so he could learn about being a **politician** (pol-ih-TISH-un). Henry worked with Elliot Richardson, who was the **secretary** (SEK-re-tehr-ee) of Health, Education, and Welfare. Richardson taught him how important politicians could be in helping cities solve their problems. He told Henry that he should return to San Antonio and work in **politics** (POL-ih-tiks).

▲ Henry moved his family back to San Antonio when he decided to work in politics. Shown here are his wife Mary Alice, his daughter, Theresa, and his son, John Paul.

A Young Councilman

In 1975, Henry won his first **election** (ih-LEK-shun). At the age of 27, he became the youngest **councilman** (KOWN-sil-man) in San Antonio's history. He was reelected in 1977 and in 1979. He worked with many groups, including Communities Organized for Public Service (COPS). COPS was a Hispanic group that worked to make better lives for Mexican Americans. Henry wanted to **improve** (im-PROOV) the lives of everyone in the city, especially the poor.

The people of San Antonio liked Henry because he cared about what was good for the city and for them. ▲

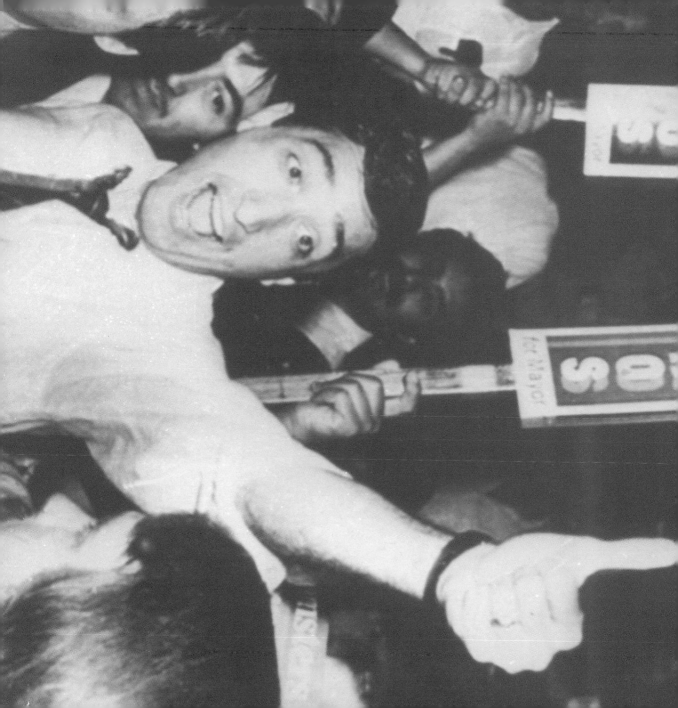

San Antonio's Mayor

In 1981, Henry was elected to the job he had wanted since college. He became mayor of San Antonio. He was the first Mexican American ever elected mayor of a big city. He was reelected three times, in 1983, 1985, and 1987. Henry believed that it was important for the city to make more money. This money could be used to do things for the people of the city, such as building homes for people who did not have them. Under Henry's leadership, San Antonio became a better city for people to live in.

▲ All of Henry's hard work paid off when he was elected mayor of San Antonio. He served as mayor for eight years.

A Great Honor

Henry was also a college **professor** (pro-FES-er). He traveled around the country talking to people about how to make cities better. In 1983, President Ronald Reagan asked Henry to be a member of a **committee** (kuh-MIT-ee) that talked about what was happening in Central America. In 1984, Walter Mondale, who was running for president, almost chose Henry to run with him. Henry was the first Mexican American to be in the running for vice president. This was a great **honor** (ON-er) for Henry.

Henry traveled around the country talking to people about how to make cities better. ▲

Working for America

In 1992, almost twenty years after Elliot Richardson had told Henry that he should become a politician, President Bill Clinton asked him to become the secretary of U.S. Housing and Urban Development. In that job, Henry used all he had learned when he helped to make San Antonio a better city. He worked to make it possible for cities all across America to have things such as better roads and better schools. He worked again toward building homes for poor people.

As secretary of U.S. Housing and Urban Development, Henry's job was to help make cities across the country better places to live.

New Projects

Henry left his job as secretary in 1997. He returned to San Antonio to work on other projects. Henry has always known what he wanted to do. And he has worked hard to make that happen. He has never forgotten his Mexican heritage. Henry Cisneros has always found a way to help Hispanic people. He once said he believes that when people have the tools to work with, they will do great things. By working together, he said, all Americans can make their country great.

Glossary

committee (kuh-MIT-ee) A group of people who meet and work toward a goal.

councilman (KOWN-sil-man) A person who works to solve a city's problems.

election (ih-LEK-shun) Choosing something by vote.

heritage (HEHR-ih-tij) Cultural traditions that are handed down from parent to child.

honor (ON-er) A source of credit or worth.

improve (im-PROOV) To make better.

journalist (JER-nul-ist) A person who gathers, writes, and presents the news in newspapers and magazines or on radio or television.

leadership (LEE-der-ship) The skill to direct other people.

mayor (MAY-er) A person who is elected to be in charge of a city.

migrant (MY-grent) A person who moves from place to place.

politician (pol-ih-TISH-un) A person who works for the government.

politics (POL-ih-tiks) The work of the government.

printer (PRIN-ter) A person who prints newspapers, magazines, or books.

professor (pro-FES-er) A teacher at a college or university.

secretary (SEK-re-tehr-ee) A person who is the head of a government department.

23

Index